EXPORTING FROM INDIA

A STEP-BY-STEP GUIDE

DR. JAGADEESH PILLAI

Made with ♥ on the Notion Press Platform
www.notionpress.com

|| Dedicated to all wisdom seekers around the world ||

Contents

Contents

Prayer

"Om Bhadram Karnebhih Shrunuyaama
DevaahBhadram Pashyemaakshabhiryajatraah
SthirairangaistushtuvaamsastanoobhihVyashema
Devahitam YadaayuhSwasti Na Indro
VridhashravaahSwasti Nah Pooshaa
VishwavedaahSwasti Nastaarkshyo ArishtanemihSwasti
No Brihaspatir DadhaatuOm Shantih, Shantih, Shantih"

The literal meaning of this mantra is: OM. O Gods! Let us hear auspicious words from our ears. O reverent Gods! Let us behold propitious visions from our eyes, let our organs and body be stable, healthy, and strong. Let us do that which is pleasing to the gods in the life span allotted to us. May Indra, inscribed in the scriptures, bring us fortune! May Pushan, the knower of the world, grant us prosperity! May Trakshya, who vanquishes enemies, bestow us with blessings! May Brihaspati bring us success!
OM Peace, Peace, Peace.

About The Author

Dr. Jagadeesh Pillai is a renowned Guinness World Record holder, writer, and researcher hailing from Varanasi, also known as the abode of Lord Shiva. With a Ph.D. in Vedic Science and a range of creative ideas and achievements, he is a true polymath. He is the author of more than 100 books including Research Publications. Although his roots can be traced back to Kerala, the people of Varanasi hold him in high regard and affectionately consider him one of their own.

In 1998, Dr. Pillai was offered a job at Banaras Hindu University, but he left the position after only two months to pursue greater goals in life. He believed that in order to study Indian scriptures and engage in other creative endeavours, he needed to retire from the daily grind of working solely for money at a young age.

He started an export business from scratch, using the knowledge he had gained from a previous job in the industry. His intelligence and unique approach to business led to great success in a short period of time, earning him more in just a decade and a half than he would have in a lifetime working in a government job. Upon the passing of Dr. APJ Abdul Kalam, Dr. Pillai decided to leave the business and dedicate himself to reading, studying, researching, and experimenting.

During his tenure in the export business, Dr. Pillai traveled to over 16 countries, gaining valuable insight and experiencing the world and life in detail.

Dr. Pillai has achieved four Guinness World Records in the following subjects:

"Script to Screen" - In this record, Dr. Pillai produced and directed an animation film within the shortest time possible, breaking the previous record set by Canadians. He has also received numerous national and international awards and recognitions for this achievement.

Longest Line of Postcards - For this record, Dr. Pillai created a line of 16,300 postcards on the occasion of the 163rd anniversary of Indian Postal Day. The event also included a questionnaire about the Indian flag.

Largest Poster Awareness Campaign - Dr. Pillai designed an awareness campaign on the subject of "Beti Bachao - Beti Padhao" (Save the Girl Child - Educate the Girl Child) to achieve this record.

Largest Envelope - In tribute to the Indian Prime Minister's "Make in India" initiative, Dr. Pillai created a 4000 square meter envelope using waste paper to achieve this record.

Attempted - **70000 Candles on a 210 kg Cake** - To celebrate the 70th Indian Independence Day, Dr. Pillai attempted to light 70,000 candles on a 210 kg cake, which was recorded in World Records India.

Attempted - **Documentary on Dhamek Stupa of Sarnath in 17 Languages** - Dr. Pillai attempted to create a documentary on the Dhamek Stupa of Sarnath, dubbing it in 17 different languages. The result of this attempt is currently awaiting confirmation from the Guinness World Records.

Dr. Pillai is skilled in teaching the Bhagavad Gita, a Hindu scripture, and is popular among young people. He has helped many young people improve their lives through his motivational teachings.

In addition to teaching, he has composed and sung numerous Sanskrit Bhajans and patriotic songs.

He has also written and directed several short films and documentaries for awareness campaigns, and has volunteered with the police in both UP and Kerala to spread awareness about various issues through videos and photography.

Incredibly, he has produced and directed over 100 documentaries about the city of Varanasi, all on his own.

He has also helped and guided more than 25 boys and girls to achieve world records through creative and innovative methods. He is a multifaceted person who uses his intellect and the blessings given to him by God to excel in various areas. He is both a teacher and a student, always learning and teaching, and is able to master any subject he comes across.

He is a selfless social activist and motivational speaker who has overcome struggles and failures to become a successful and enthusiastic individual with a rich life experience.

In addition to his work with the Bhagavad Gita, he is also

an efficient Tarot card reader, Astro-Vastu consultant, and a talented singer and composer. He has sung the entire Ram Charita Manas and Bhagavad Gita in his own compositions, and has sung the phrase "Lokah Samastha Sukhino Bhavantu" in 50 different languages. He is currently working on a detailed and scientific study of Vedas, Upanishads, Puranas, and the Bhagavad Gita. He has also composed and sung the Hanuman Chalisa and Gayatri Mantra in 108 and 1008 different compositions, respectively.

Awards - Four Times Guinness World Records, Winner of Mahatma Gandhi Vishwa Shanti Puraskar, Mahatma Gandhi Global Peace Ambassador, Kashi Ratna Award, Dr. APJ Abdul Kalam Motivational Person of the Year 2017, Mother Teresa Award, Indira Gandhi Priyadarshini Award, Bharat Vikas Ratna Award, Udyog Ratna Award, Vigyan Prasar Award, Poorvanchal Ratn Samman.

Preface

Exporting from India: A Step-by-Step Guide is a comprehensive guide to the process of exporting goods from India. It provides readers with a detailed overview of the various steps involved in the process, from understanding the regulations and paperwork to finding the right buyers and negotiating the best deals.

This book is an invaluable resource for anyone looking to export from India. It is written in an easy-to-understand language and provides a wealth of information on the subject. It covers topics such as the legal and regulatory framework, the different types of export products, the various methods of payment, and the different types of buyers. It also provides tips and advice on how to maximize profits and minimize risks.

Exporting from India: A Step-by-Step Guide is an essential guide for anyone looking to export from India. It is a comprehensive and detailed guide that will help readers understand the process and make informed decisions. It is written in a clear and concise manner and provides readers with the necessary information to make the most of their export opportunities. This book is a must-have for anyone looking to export from India.

CHAPTER ONE

Introduction to Exporting from India

The process of exporting goods from India has grown more complex as globalization has made international trade more accessible and important. Exporting can be intimidating for a small business in India, but understanding the basic process and the steps necessary to carry out successful transactions will ensure success in your international trade. In this essay, we will discuss how to start exporting from India, the key steps to consider, the various regulations imposed by the government of India, and the relevant bodies that oversee export efforts in India.

International trade is critical to economies across the world, and India's export industry plays an important role in providing numerous goods and services to the global market. The government of India regulates the export sector through a number of agencies and organizations in order to streamline the process and ensure compliance with national law. If you are interested in starting up an export business in India, the first step is to familiarize yourself with the Export and Import regulations of India (Exim policy). This policy is available on the Government of India's website and outlines the rules and regulations for the export of goods from India and their import into different countries.

The next step is to identify your target market and determine the best way to access it. This may entail setting up a website, registering with potential trade partners in the target country, or mapping out the routes or means of delivery. In addition, it is necessary to explore the export and import regulations of the target country and find ways to abide by the regulations to ensure efficient and smooth transactions.

Once you have fully understood the regulations in both India and the target country and are ready to start your export business, you will need to open a bank account specifically for your international trade transactions. This account should be in a currency that is accepted as payment by buyers in the target country or region and will make all financial transactions much easier. From here, you will need to identify potential buyers, start trading, and advertise your services, to create awareness in the target country.

The Indian government also provides various subsidies and incentives to facilitate exports from India. These include the Merchandise Exports from India Scheme (MEIS) that provide a benefit for eligible exports, the Export Promotion Capital Goods (EPCG) scheme that allows the import of capital goods for export-related activities, and the Export-Oriented Units (EOU) scheme which permits the operation of units for export-oriented production. As such, each of these schemes can assist in reducing export costs and promoting trade from India.

The Export Credit Guarantee Corporation (ECGC) is an organization that provides export credit insurance to Indian exporters, helping them protect themselves against the risks associated with international trade, such as credit risk and contract breaches by foreign buyers. Moreover, the Reserve Bank of India (RBI) sets limits on certain items to ensure the safety of Indian exporters. As a result, exporting from India has become an increasingly intricate endeavor, requiring a comprehensive understanding of the various risks and regulations involved.

CHAPTER TWO

IDENTIFYING AND SELECTING EXPORT PRODUCTS

In the current age of globalization, companies can greatly expand their customer base by exporting their products. Identifying and selecting the right export products is essential to running a sustainable and successful export business. Companies can identify new export opportunities by thinking creatively and using market research. Founders need to carefully assess the potential of each export market by utilizing the right resources and assessing customer needs in those markets. Once export markets have been identified, companies need to select the right export products to start the export business.

The first step to selecting export products is to analyze the customer needs in each identified export market; this will help the company find export products that are likely to be successful in that market. Companies should use market research to understand these customer needs and consider customer demographics, cultural nuances, preferences, trends, and price points. Examining customer purchasing habits can help identify customer needs and help to optimize sales strategies.

In addition to understanding customer needs, export products should also have strategic value for the company. This includes examining the market demand and the anticipated return on investment to ensure the product is worth the effort and associated costs of exporting it. Companies should also consider the product's design, quality, and costs; understanding the production and distribution costs, legal requirements, and the need for additional support. It is important to research competitors in the export market, as this can give an insight into how competitive the product may be.

Finally, companies should develop a marketing strategy to attract customers and maximize sales. This includes creating an effective communication and distribution channel to effectively reach customers, as well as unique competitive strategies to stand out from competitors. This could include promoting the product's value, developing loyalty programs, or offering discounts and promotional campaigns to boost sales.

Identifying and selecting export products is a crucial step to the success of any export business. Companies should take the time to thoroughly research export markets, customer needs, and potential product success, as well as carefully consider the associated costs and strategic value before investing in any product. Then, developing an effective marketing strategy to attract customers and maximize sales is necessary to ensure successful export operations.

CHAPTER THREE

Procurement and Sourcing Strategies

Procurement and sourcing strategies are integral components of any new export business. Though there are several key aspects of any export business, like marketing, finance, and legal protection, neglecting these two areas can lead to large-scale losses and even potential bankruptcy. Therefore, devising a sound procurement and sourcing strategy should be a priority for any business looking to enter the export market.

First, proper procurement techniques should be established in order to ensure that the raw materials required are available to create the necessary end product. Businesses must identify reliable and capable suppliers who meet their specific requirements for quality, price, and delivery times. Once potential suppliers have been identified, proper due diligence is necessary to ensure that a relationship is established that benefits both parties. It is also important to consider the geographical area of the suppliers in order to capitalize on cost savings and reduce delivery times.

Second, sourcing strategies should be designed to obtain the necessary raw materials and products required to produce the finished good. Companies must analyze the cost of products in different locations and compare it to their own budget in order to select the most cost-effective supply options. Additionally, international sourcing can provide significant cost savings while increasing product quality by allowing businesses to purchase from nations with specialized manufacturing capabilities.

Furthermore, companies must consider risk management when obtaining products and materials. Factors including shipment size, delivery time, and the political environment of the supplier country should be taken into account to minimize the potential for disruption during the shipping process. Lastly, businesses must ensure that all suppliers and product lines have certificates of origin and comply with export laws in order to prevent any customs delays and ensure successful entry on the market.

A strong and sound procurement and sourcing strategy are fundamental for any business looking to establish an export business. Careful research and risk analysis must be conducted in order to create an effective plan that operates through reliable supply chains and meets the necessary standards for successful entry on the export market.

CHAPTER FOUR

LEGAL AND COMPLIANCE REQUIREMENTS FOR EXPORTING

Exporting businesses face an arduous set of legal and compliance requirements. Processes pertaining to any company's export and import of goods, services, and technology to or from another country must comply with the regulations of each country's governments, as well as international standards to ensure that business practices are managed safely, ethically and in accordance with trading countries' prohibitions, restrictions and mandates.

One of the key considerations when dealing with international business relates to import and export regulations. Depending on the specific products being exported and where they're being shipped, there may be a set of legal codes, tariffs and restrictions associated with the industry or objects themselves. This can include export license restrictions, export control regulations and sanctions. In most cases, having a sufficiently detailed shipping document and contract will ensure a smooth shipment and avoid potential fines or other legal implications.

In addition to export/import laws, businesses must also consider country-specific laws as well as international regulations. For example, trade agreements between two countries can impose restrictions on the types of raw materials or components that can be used in the product. Country-specific taxes, tariffs and other fees may also apply.

Businesses exporting products may also be required to follow a specific set of ethical standards. For example, businesses must ensure that their product or service adheres to international labor, environmental and human rights standards. Similarly, companies must demonstrate their commitment to fair practices with respect to foreign tenders as well as taxation. Companies are also responsible for data and cybersecurity, as personal information could be exploited if it is not properly secured.

Finally, companies should be aware of the trade sanctions, embargos and economic boycotts that are in place in various countries and communities. Companies must comply with all applicable sanctions and ensure that none of their purchased or produced items originate in any areas subject to such measures. Failure to comply could result in hefty fines or penalties and irreparable damage to the international reputation of the company.

Exporting businesses must take a wide range of legal and compliance requirements into account when conducting business around the globe. Export/import regulations, taxes, ethical standards, trade agreements, sanctions and embargos are just some of the considerations businesses must take into account to stay compliant. A thorough understanding of these requirements is essential for businesses that wish to succeed in international trade.

CHAPTER FIVE

OBTAINING EXPORT LICENSES AND PERMITS

Legal requirements are important to consider when a company is interested in exporting goods from India. Export licenses and permits in India must be obtained in order to properly export goods to other countries. Failure to comply with the country's export regulations can lead to significant delays and legal sanctions, so it is especially important that one understands the process of obtaining the necessary export license and permit before exporting goods.

The first step in obtaining an export license and permit is to identify relevant export regulations. Depending on the type of product, one may need to register their products with the Indian government and obtain export clearance. The Indian government has a host of agencies and government bodies that oversee the export of certain goods. For example, fish, animals, and animal products must receive clearance from the Department of Animal Husbandry, Dairying, and Fisheries or the Department of Agriculture. Export of pharmaceuticals must receive clearance from the Drugs Controller General of India. Other products must obtain clearance from the relevant department in the Indian government.

Once the relevant jurisdictional body has been identified, the next step is to apply for the necessary export licenses and permits. It is important to note that several documents must be submitted along with the application. The export license and permit application will require basic company-specific information such as company name, address, registration number, and IEC (Importer Exporter Code). In addition to these documents, information regarding product details such as item description, HS code, country of origin and other details will also have to be submitted. Depending on the type of product, other documents such as quality certificates may also have to be sent along with the application.

Once the application has been submitted, an acknowledgement receipt will be issued. After the acknowledgement receipt has been issued, the application will be reviewed and, if necessary, additional documents may be requested by the licensing authority. Once the review is complete and all necessary documents have been submitted, the export license and permit will be issued.

It is important to understand the process for obtaining export licenses and permits before exporting goods from India. Before beginning the process, one should have a comprehensive understanding of the product they are exporting, the jurisdictional body that oversees the product, and the relevant documentation that must accompany their application. Following the correct process and completing all necessary steps will ensure that the export of goods from India is conducted in accordance with local laws.

CHAPTER SIX

INCOTERMS AND PAYMENT TERMS

An export business pursuant to Indian law comprises of several terms and conditions, which derives its significance from the proper functioning of the business and avoidance of disputes. The two important terms that can make or break an export business are Incoterms and Payment Terms.

Incoterms, short for International Commercial Terms, are a set of rules published and developed by International Trade Commission (ITC) to govern the responsibilities and liabilities of parties related to import and export of goods. They are the standardised trade terms and of particular relevance in determining how international trade transactions should be structured, and help in eliminating any misinterpretation of rights and liabilities among the parties. The common Incoterms in India are FOB (Free on Board), CFR (Cost and Freight), CIF (Cost, Insurance & Freight), CPT (Carriage Paid to), DAP (Delivered at Place), DDP (Delivered Duty Paid), and EXW (Ex-works).

The other crucial element for any export business is Payment Terms. It is of great importance to determine the payment terms prior to the commencement of any export transaction, as it sets out the responsibilities and liabilities of each party. Payment mechanisms accepted in India for exports are cash against documents, bills for collection, letters of credit, open account, and the combination of these payment mechanisms.

While cash against documents requires payment upon obtaining documents relating to goods, bills for collection requires payment to be made on collection of documents of goods. Letters of credit are agreements typically used in sales between two parties, wherein one party (seller) promises to provide goods and other party (buyer) promises to make payment upon delivery. Open account payment terms are based on understanding between two parties (seller and buyer) wherein the buyer agrees to pay the seller within a stipulated time period.

Understanding and abiding by Incoterms and Payment Terms is essential for any export business in India. It is necessary for the parties to understand and agree upon the same in writing, which would further help in having a well secured and prosperous export business.

CHAPTER SEVEN

Freight Forwarding and Logistics

India has an abundance of untapped potential in the global market, making it an attractive destination for entrepreneurs who are looking to start an export business. Yet, it takes a great deal of planning and foresight to overcome the logistical challenges associated with exporting goods from India to foreign markets. This is where freight forwarding and logistics can help.

Freight forwarding and logistics are the process of coordinating and managing the transportation of goods from one point to another. This could include sea, air, or train services, depending on the nature of the goods being exported. Logistic services include everything from helping to prepare customs documents to tracking the transportation chain so that packages are not lost in transit.

By using freight forwarding and logistics, manufacturers

can save time and money when starting an export business. For example, freight forwarders are experts in processing customs documents and ensuring that items are shipped in the most efficient way. This can cut down on unnecessary delays and fees associated with incorrect shipping. The knowledge of the freight forwarding team can also be invaluable when trying to choose the best route for the transit of certain goods.

Moreover, it helps expedite the process of exporting items from India, which can be complicated because of the varied customs regulations in place. In addition to this, freight forwarders can provide support for financing and insurance for shipments, providing peace of mind for newcomers to exporting.

Thanks to solutions such as freight forwarding and logistics, India has the potential to become a major export destination. Manufacturers and entrepreneurs can capitalize on this potential by taking advantage of the services offered by freight forwarders. They ensure that goods are shipped in the fastest, safest, and cost effective way, providing a strong foundation for getting started in the world of international trade.

CHAPTER EIGHT

CUSTOMS CLEARANCE AND DOCUMENTATION

Exporting goods from India is a major contributor to its economy. Each country has its own laws and regulations governing the sale and export of goods, and India is no exception. These laws and regulations can be very complex and it is important for entrepreneurs and businesses to understand how to navigate them in order to export goods. Customs clearance and documentation plays a major role in the export process, and understanding this process is essential for successfully starting an export business in India.

Customs clearance involves verifying and validating the documents associated with an export shipment, making sure that all required documentation is in order and that the goods being exported are legally allowed to be exported for the destination. All export related documents should be presented to customs officers, and all required fees and taxes must be paid in order to receive the necessary customs clearance. Depending on the type of goods being exported, additional documents may be required such as certificates of origin, bill of lading, export license, and special permits.

When it comes to documentation, all export documents must be prepared and maintained accurately and accurately according to the guidelines of the government. All necessary paperwork such as invoices, bills of lading, and documents of export clearance and payment have to be submitted to customs authorities. In addition, banks may also have their own set of requirements such as letters of credit or export advances. It is critical for business owners and entrepreneurs to understand these requirements and ensure that all documentation is complete and correct before submitting it to authorities.

It is important to note that the export process in India is heavily regulated and can change from year to year. It is advisable to research the latest regulations and policies before and while starting an export business. It is also important to consult with an experienced attorney or accountant to ensure that all legal requirements are being met and to minimize the risks involved in the export process.

With the right preparation and documentation, entrepreneurs and businesses can confidently and legally begin trading in the global market. By understanding the customs clearance and documentation process, businesses can ensure that their export journey will be smooth and prosperous.

CHAPTER NINE

EXPORT PRICING AND QUOTATIONS

India is a major exporter of various goods and services, making it an important sector in the economy. Export pricing and quotations are an important element of the export cycle and play a pivotal role in making a sale. Export pricing and quotations are vital to the success of Indian businesses in the global market.

Export pricing and quotations are the process of determining the final price of the goods or services being exported. It is important to establish a fair and realistic price so that international customers perceive a product or service as valuable. Establishing a good price depends on a variety of factors such as market conditions, quality of the product, any discounts, type of customer, and competition from other exporters. All of these aspects determine the export pricing and how attractive it is for the customer.

In India, the Ministry of Commerce and Industry along with the Director General of Foreign Trade is responsible for the regulation of export prices. These organizations determine the export policy and ensure the fair pricing of the goods and services being exported. Exporters must comply with export pricing regulations set by the government in order to be successful. Compliance is achieved by preparing quotes and price lists in a timely manner.

Quotes and price lists should include all costs associated with the product including labor charges, shipping and handling fees, and any tariffs or duties that may apply. The price should also be broken down line-by-line to ensure complete transparency. This way, customers can clearly see what they are paying for and can make an informed decision. It is also important to ensure that all quotes and price lists adhere to any relevant industry/product certifications.

Finally, exporters should also be aware of any export incentives that may be offered to them. Exporters are often eligible for tax credits, tariff exemptions, and other incentives from the government that can help to lower the overall costs associated with exports.

Export pricing and quotations play an important role in the success of export businesses in India. Establishing a fair market price is vital to making a sale, as customers need to perceive the product or service to be of value. It is important to understand factors such as market conditions, quality of the product, discounts, customer type and competition when formulating export prices. Additionally, exporters must be compliant with export pricing regulations set by the government and prepare quotes and price lists that include all associated charges. As long as exporters understand these elements, they will be able to price their products and services properly and be successful in international export markets.

CHAPTER TEN

MARKETING AND PROMOTION STRATEGIES

Marketing and promotion strategies are essential for any organization intending to start export. Exporting requires different strategies than what is required on domestic market. As such, business owners, marketing teams and other pertinent stakeholders must plan and create effective strategies to ensure that their exports become successful. Therefore, this paper will provide an insight into how to create effective strategies to start exports from India.

The first step to create successful marketing strategies to start exports from India is to clearly define what the business offers. Doing so will enable the team to draft a well-defined mission statement. The mission should include the type of products, the target market for exports, and the desired outcome of the exports. Further, a headline statement can be created to serve as the driving force behind the promotional strategy. Doing so will enable the team to focus on objectives needed to maintain brand visibility and market exposure.

Next, business owners and marketing teams must conduct comprehensive market research to determine the needs and wants of the target market. This should involve examining competition, global trade laws, and potential trade partners. Market research should also be used to inform promotions and create effective marketing messages that can help create a memorable, unique brand. By doing so, the organization can focus on spreading brand exposure to influence both local and international trade partners.

In addition, to effectively promote exports from India, organizations should consider advertising in international publications and digital spaces. This will enable them to target international audiences and can help increase brand exposure. It is also wise to use social media to promote the brand's mission and values through creative content. Social media can be used to engage with international markets, creating a space for customers to interact with the organization and provide feedback.

Finally, getting the right mix of the correct export items can help promote exports from India. For instance, products like jewelry, spices, and textiles are popular items that have a high demand in foreign markets. Focus should be on identifying best-selling products and consulting buyers to get insights about potential prospects. Further, pursuing certifications for quality and safety can help make export products more in-demand.

When a business is about to start export from India, marketing strategies must be carefully planned to ensure success. Comprehensive market research, crafting of effective messages, advertising, and targeting the right mix of products are all key strategies in ensuring the success of imports. Do these strategies well, and the exports from India will be successful.

CHAPTER ELEVEN

TRADE SHOWS AND EXHIBITIONS

Exhibitions, Trade Shows and Fairs are great platforms to promote one's products, services and ideas, especially when it comes to starting an export business in India. Today, the Indian domestic markets are becoming progressively saturated with similar products and services that have made it increasingly difficult for entrepreneurs to differentiate their offerings and clear a market for themselves. Hence, brining one's products and services to an international audience has become a reliable and effective way to stand out from the competition and exponentially increase one's business prospects.

With that being said, Trade Shows and Exhibitions remain one of the best opportunities for Indian entrepreneurs to take their business to the next level. Exhibitions offer a platform to present products and services to potential buyers from the international market, and serve as a great opportunity to create networks and initiate deals. Furthermore, a large amount of buyers attend these events from the international arena, allowing businesses to meet buyers from multiple countries at a single destination.

Additionally, these events also offer prospects to make great connections with major importers, distributors and other professionals in the industry. This also allows businesses to gain an insight of the market in terms of price sensitivity and customer preferences, making it easier to cater to the customer's needs accordingly. Additionally, the international platform offers resourceful information regarding tax, customs and international payment terms, giving presentations a competitive edge. On top of that, the opportunity to showcase product specifications and performance tests in front of an international audience serves as a great way to create a brand identity.

Finally, Trade Shows and Exhibitions also offer a great way to establish one's image and presence in the international market. Along with connecting with potential buyers and receiving feedback, these events also provide a great chance to initiate business relationships for future success. Furthermore, there is a great potential to generate sales, gain international exposure and set up a successful export business in India.

Therefore, Trade Shows and Exhibitions present a great opportunity for aspiring entrepreneurs in India to expand their business prospects in the international market. By offering potential buyers the chance to see the products and services presented, these events create a great platform to create a network, initiate deals and gain recognition in the international market. This step is essential to kick-start one's business and establish a strong footprint in the international market.

CHAPTER TWELVE

ONLINE MARKETING AND E-COMMERCE

Traditional routes of advertising have been rapidly replaced by innovative digital marketing techniques, making it easier for businesses to penetrate new markets and export their product or service to other countries.In the wake of this changing landscape, India has also seen a surge in its e-commerce and online marketing industry, with exports of products and services from India more than quadrupling in the last 10 years.

Online marketing is defined as the process of promoting a product or service on the Internet using various digital channels such as search engines, social media, and email. It has become increasingly popular as it enables businesses to target customers in a much wider and more cost-effective manner than traditional advertising methods.

For Indian businesses looking to export to foreign markets,

the benefits of online marketing are quite evident. The Internet is a global marketplace, allowing them to reach out to a much wider audience around the world, including potential buyers from next door or from across the other side of the world. This opens up vast opportunities for businesses to expand their reach and tap into new markets, which could potentially bring in a great deal of revenue. Furthermore, as more and more Indian businesses have come to understand the technological advancements in the domain of digital marketing, the costs associated with international marketing have reduced significantly, making it far more accessible for organisations that cannot afford traditional forms of advertising.

E-commerce has become an integral part of the online marketing industry, representing the online buying and selling of products. Indian businesses have greatly benefitted from the increased demand for online purchases, especially in an increasingly digitized world where customers are increasingly switching their purchases to online platforms. Businesses receive payment in a very secure and efficient manner, directly through a wide range of online payment gateways and other solutions, enabling them to access global markets while avoiding potential hassle to export through traditional methods.

E-commerce also helps start-ups and small businesses to set up shop in other countries by providing them with the necessary framework and infrastructure required to get off the ground. This makes it easier and much less expensive for them to establish a foot in the global market, which could help them expand exponentially in the long term.

The growth of India's e-commerce and online marketing industry has enabled businesses to better compete in the international market, helping them to penetrate new markets with reduced expenditure and time. Therefore, for businesses looking to export from India, these are highly beneficial tools to use.

CHAPTER THIRTEEN

Building and Managing Export Teams

Export teams play an important role in the international business of any large or small company, and the process of building and managing these teams can be complex but extremely rewarding. If a company is looking to start exporting from India, they must build a team of dedicated individuals to ensure the success of their export venture.

The first step in building the export team is to identify the most suitable candidates for the job. With the current shortage of skilled talent in India, it is important to find the most qualified and experienced personnel who have a thorough understanding of international trade and the laws associated with it. The team should include a variety of people with different backgrounds in order to cover all aspects of the export operation. This could include managers, agents and distributors, lawyers, accountants, freight forwarders, and other export and logistics specialists.

Once the team has been assembled, it is important to ensure that all members have an understanding of their roles and responsibilities. It is vital for each individual to have a comprehensive understanding of company policy, and to be aware of their specific roles in achieving a successful export operation. The team should be briefed on the company's aims and goals, and they should be able to provide regular feedback on performance to the management.

To manage the team efficiently, it is important to establish clear lines of communication between the members and the management. This will enable the team to work towards the common goals of the organization, without the risk of confusion arising or important tasks being overlooked. Each member of the team should attend regular meetings to discuss progress, and feedback should be sought in order to identify and address any problems that may arise.

Finally, it is important to recognise the efforts and achievements of the export team. Rewards should be given for successful projects, and recognition should be provided for exemplary work. This will motivate the team to continue to work towards the success of the export operations, and will ensure that the team remains motivated and productive.

Building and managing an export team is a complex but rewarding task. Companies looking to start exporting from India must find qualified personnel with a thorough understanding of international trade, and must ensure that all team members are aware of their responsibilities. Clear communication lines should be established between the members of the export team and the management, and rewards should be given to the team for successful projects. By taking these steps, companies can ensure the success of their export venture.

CHAPTER FOURTEEN

INTERNATIONAL MARKET RESEARCH AND ANALYSIS

India, with over 1.25 billion people, has one of the largest and fastest-growing economies in the world, with a large number of potential customers for Indian exporters. For any business that is looking to expand into international markets, it is important to conduct thorough research and analysis to ensure the success of the venture.

When researching potential markets and products to export from India, it is important to consider various factors including political, economic, and social factors as well as geographical and competitive factors. Political, economic and social factors could have an impact on the business's ability to enter into a particular market and therefore need to be taken into account. For example, in the case of the US market, tariffs and other trade barriers may affect the competitiveness of Indian products.

Geographical aspects should also be considered when conducting market research and analysis. This includes studying the region in which a product will be exported, the transportation costs associated with this and the population of the area. In addition, demographics such as age, income, and educational levels should also be studied to determine the target market for a particular product.

Finally, a thorough analysis of the competitive environment should be undertaken to understand the dynamics of the market and the presence of any potential competitors. This may include studying the competitors' pricing strategies, advertising campaigns, and customer service. Additionally, understanding any existing legal or regulatory constraints that may limit a product's success in the international market should also be evaluated.

When evaluating these factors to begin exporting from India, it is vital to remember that the key to success is understanding the target market. As such, conducting thorough market research and analysis is essential to ensure that the venture is successful. In addition, it is also important to consider the suitability of the product and its ability to meet the needs of the customers in the target market. Once the research has been conducted and the export business is developed, it is important to continuously monitor the market and make changes as needed.

CHAPTER FIFTEEN

Identifying and Entering New Markets

Identifying and entering new markets is an extremely important area of focus for export businesses in India. Indian exports are an integral part of the Indian economy, as they not only provide foreign exchange income but also increase the competitiveness of the Indian manufacturing industry. Companies need to be able to identify and exploit new markets in order to maximize their chances of success when selling abroad.

The first step for a prospective Indian exporter is to identify the target countries for export. Depending on the product or service being exported, different countries may be more suitable. Factors such as market size, economic stability, and cultural affinity all play a part in choosing potential new export markets. It is also important to assess competitors currently operating in the target markets, so that a new entrant is aware of any existing competition and the associated challenges.

Once an exporter has identified the target countries, they should research the local laws and regulations governing exports, as well as the import taxation policies. They should also investigate the distribution channels available in each country, and the most appropriate ones for their product or service, as well as understanding the local consumer demand.

In order to enter a new market, exporters must ensure all of the necessary paperwork is in place, including obtaining visas and any necessary permits or licenses. They should also ensure that their product meets the local regulatory and safety standards – a vital step for successful exporting.

Finally, exporters must plan their promotional and marketing activities for the target countries. Advertising in print and electronic media, creating content for websites and social media channels, and using other promotional techniques can all help to build the brand of an Indian exporter and introduce it to potential customers in the target countries.

An effective export strategy is vital for businesses looking to enter new markets. It is important that prospective exporters conduct thorough research and planning prior to entering any new market, to ensure their success in the target countries. By taking the right steps up front, exporters can boost their chances of success when exporting from India.

CHAPTER SIXTEEN

BUILDING AND MANAGING INTERNATIONAL RELATIONSHIPS

Export teams play an important role in the international business of any large or small company, and the process of building and managing these teams can be complex but extremely rewarding. If a company is looking to start exporting from India, they must build a team of dedicated individuals to ensure the success of their export venture.

The first step in building the export team is to identify the most suitable candidates for the job. With the current shortage of skilled talent in India, it is important to find the most qualified and experienced personnel who have a thorough understanding of international trade and the laws associated with it. The team should include a variety of people with different backgrounds in order to cover all aspects of the export operation. This could include managers, agents and distributors, lawyers, accountants, freight forwarders, and other export and logistics specialists.

Once the team has been assembled, it is important to ensure that all members have an understanding of their roles and responsibilities. It is vital for each individual to have a comprehensive understanding of company policy, and to be aware of their specific roles in achieving a successful export operation. The team should be briefed on the company's aims and goals, and they should be able to provide regular feedback on performance to the management.

To manage the team efficiently, it is important to establish clear lines of communication between the members and the management. This will enable the team to work towards the common goals of the organization, without the risk of confusion arising or important tasks being overlooked. Each member of the team should attend regular meetings to discuss progress, and feedback should be sought in order to identify and address any problems that may arise.

Finally, it is important to recognise the efforts and achievements of the export team. Rewards should be given for successful projects, and recognition should be provided for exemplary work. This will motivate the team to continue to work towards the success of the export operations, and will ensure that the team remains motivated and productive.

Building and managing an export team is a complex but rewarding task. Companies looking to start exporting from

India must find qualified personnel with a thorough understanding of international trade, and must ensure that all team members are aware of their responsibilities. Clear communication lines should be established between the members of the export team and the management, and rewards should be given to the team for successful projects. By taking these steps, companies can ensure the success of their export venture.

Cultural Intelligence and Cross-cultural Management

India is a culturally diverse nation, and understanding the nuances of its culture is essential for successful exporting. Cultural intelligence (CQ) is the ability to understand, appreciate, and interact with people from different cultures. Cross-cultural management is the practice of managing people from different cultures in a way that is respectful and effective. When it comes to exporting from India, having a strong understanding of CQ and cross-cultural management is essential for success.

CQ is a key factor in understanding the cultural nuances of India. It involves being aware of the different values, beliefs, and customs of the people in India, and being able to adjust one's behavior accordingly. This includes being able to recognize and respect the different languages, religions, and social norms of the people in India. It also involves being able to communicate effectively with people from different cultures, and being able to adjust one's communication style to be more effective.

Cross-cultural management is also important for successful exporting from India. This involves understanding the different cultural values and beliefs of the people in India, and being able to manage them in a way that is respectful and effective. This includes being able to recognize and respect the different languages, religions, and social norms of the people in India, as well as being able to adjust one's management style to be more effective. It also involves being able to communicate effectively with people from different cultures, and being able to adjust one's communication style to be more effective.

Exporting from India necessitates a comprehensive comprehension of cultural intelligence and cross-cultural management. It is essential to be cognizant of the various values, beliefs, and customs of the people in India, and to be able to modify one's behavior accordingly. Moreover, it is imperative to be able to identify and honor the various languages, religions, and social conventions of the people in India, as this will enable one to effectively navigate the complexities of the Indian market. Understanding the nuances of the Indian culture is essential for any business looking to export from India, as it will enable them to build strong relationships with their Indian counterparts and ensure a successful venture.

CHAPTER EIGHTEEN

Intellectual Property and Trademark Protection

Intellectual property and trademarks are essential components of any successful export business, as they provide legal protection for the products and services being exported. In India, intellectual property and trademark protection are governed by the Indian Patents Act, 1970, and the Trade Marks Act, 1999. These laws provide a framework for protecting the rights of inventors, creators, and owners of intellectual property and trademarks.

When exporting from India, it is important to understand the legal implications of intellectual property and trademark protection. This includes understanding the scope of protection, the registration process, and the enforcement of rights. Additionally, it is important to be aware of the potential risks associated with exporting without proper protection. For example, without proper protection, a company may be exposed to the risk of counterfeiting, infringement, or other forms of unfair competition.

In addition to understanding the legal implications of intellectual property and trademark protection, it is also important to consider the economic benefits of such protection. By protecting intellectual property and trademarks, companies can ensure that their products and services are unique and distinguishable from those of their competitors. This can lead to increased sales and profits, as well as greater brand recognition and loyalty.

Finally, it is important to consider the ethical implications of intellectual property and trademark protection. Companies should strive to ensure that their products and services are not infringing on the rights of others. Additionally, companies should be aware of the potential for exploitation of intellectual property and trademarks, and should take steps to prevent such exploitation.

Intellectual property and trademark protection are essential components of any successful export business. It is important to understand the legal, economic, and ethical implications of such protection, and to take steps to ensure that the rights of inventors, creators, and owners of intellectual property and trademarks are respected. By taking the time to carefully craft their products and services, companies can ensure that they are unique and distinguishable from those of their competitors.

This can be achieved through the implementation of

innovative ideas, the use of cutting-edge technology, and the dedication to providing the highest quality of customer service. By doing so, companies can stand out from the crowd and create a lasting impression on their customers.

CHAPTER NINETEEN

FOREIGN EXCHANGE AND CURRENCY RISK MANAGEMENT

Foreign exchange and currency risk management strategies are the tools used by businesses to manage the risks related to their international dealings in terms of exchange rates and fluctuations in the value of currencies. For Indian businesses that export goods and services outside the country, foreign exchange and currency risk management is even more important, as the movement of currency markets can significantly impact profitability.

When a business exporting from India deals in a foreign currency, it is subject to the risk that their product or service may get more expensive or cheaper due to fluctuations in exchange rate. To hedge against this risk, one of the most common strategies employed is to use forward contracts. Forward contracts are an agreement between two parties to exchange two currencies with a predetermined rate in the future, allowing exporters to secure the rate for their goods now, even if the rate of exchange changes in the future. Expanding on this, exporters are also able to use options contracts, which gives them the right but not the obligation to exchange currencies at a certain rate in the future.

Another important strategy used for foreign exchange and currency risk management is hedging against fluctuation in interest rates of different currencies. This involves using debt to borrow in foreign currencies, as it offers businesses an opportunity to protect against a potential rise of their currency interest rate.

Businesses can also hedge against risks related to currency devaluation. This can be done through purchasing currency futures, which are contracts that allow exporters to buy or sell a certain amount of a currency at a fixed rate sometime in the future. This gives the exporter the option to buy or incur contracts at a future date when it may be advantageous.

Managing the risks associated with exporting from India is a key strategy for businesses to protect their profit margins and ensure their long-term financial stability. The strategies such as forward contracts, options contracts, borrowing in foreign currencies, and futures can all offer reasonable protection against adverse foreign exchange and currency rates. However, it is important for businesses to understand the risks involved, evaluate the strategies carefully, and make sure they are engaging with a reputable and reliable financial services provider to ensure that their risk management strategies deliver the desired outcomes.

CHAPTER TWENTY

Export Financing and Insurance

Export Financing & Insurance are two key elements of expanding into international markets. They are of crucial importance when it comes to a successful export venture from India.

Export Financing refers to the financial system in place to assist exporters in raising funds for their export operations. It involves the use of credit instruments like loans, invoice factoring, and documentary credits, to enable them to access funds in order to the finance goods and services being exported. This forms the cornerstone of most transactions as exporters need access to the necessary funds to purchase, store and ship goods to their intended buyers.

Export Insurance is designed to protect exporters from a range of external financial and economic risks that arise from foreign exchange rate fluctuations, payment defaults and other uncertain market conditions. Insurance policies can be designed to protect against these risks, allowing exporters to be better prepared for these eventualities and mitigate their losses in the event of an unforeseen occurrence.

In India, the Export Credit Guarantee Corporation (ECGC) of India is the main organisation that provides export finance and insurance services. It was established in 1957 to promote exports by indemnifying the risks associated with exports. The ECGC offers a wide range of products, such as credit insurance policies, performance bonds, warranty cover and political risk cover. It also provides financial assistance to exporters in the form of working capital loans, term loans, and overseas guarantees and Bonds.

Over the years, the Government of India has established various policies and schemes to facilitate the growth of Indian exports, such as the Merchandise Exports from India Scheme (MEIS), the Service Export from India Scheme (SEIS) and the Export Credit Guarantee Scheme (ECGS). These initiatives have helped Indian exporters access necessary funds and insurance cover in order to increase exports and expand their business into global markets.

Export Financing and Insurance are pivotal in allowing exporters to access finance to purchase, store and ship goods, as well as protect them from external risks due to market conditions. The ECGC of India, as well as the various policies and schemes devised by the Government of India, enhance the overall prospects of the export industry, allowing Indian exporters to participate in an ever more competitive global market.

CHAPTER TWENTY-ONE

QUALITY CONTROL AND STANDARDS

The importance of quality control and standards when exporting from India is essential to guarantee consumer health, safety and satisfaction. Quality control measures and standards help to guarantee that the products are safe for consumers, are up to the company's quality standards and meet legal requirements. Understanding the role of both quality control and standards in the export process is necessary to make sure a successful export experience.

When it comes to quality control, export items must be inspected when leaving the production facility in order to ensure that they are of the best quality for consumers. Indian export items should meet industry standards, customer requirements and international standards set by the the Association of Indian Exporters (AIE). It is important to plan appropriate steps to ensure that the items that leave the production facility adhere to these standards and are safe for consumers. This can include having an independent third-party inspection company come in and inspect the items before they are shipped to their destination.

In addition to quality control, it's important to ensure that exports meet certain standards set by the customer and the international community. For instance, exports must meet the Indian government's framework and policies, including import-export regulations, export standards, and export certifications. Items should also be compliant with any applicable trademarks and patents of the receiving country. The company should be careful to check that the exported items are suitable for the market they will be sold in.

Finally, it's important to make sure that the items on the export manifests match the items that were inspected and certified during the quality control process. When preparing an export cargo, companies must also keep detailed records for each item, including information about the manufacturer, producer, shipments and importer.

Good quality control and standards are essential for successful exporting. Companies should take the time to understand the legal requirements and industry standards that apply to their export items, as well as make sure that the items are in line with customer requirements and international standards. Taking the time to do the necessary quality control checks and make sure that the exported items match the export manifests will help ensure the successful import-export process.

CHAPTER TWENTY-TWO

Compliance with International Standards and Regulations

India has great potential as an exporting country and is a potential leader in global trade. In recent years, the government of India has made significant strides in increasing its exports, with exports accounting for more than 19% of the nation's Gross Domestic Product in recent years. The government of India has instituted a number of support and resources for exporters, which greatly help exporters in achieving their objectives.

In order to start and accelerate export operations, exporters need various resources such as finance, information, technology, and market access. To cater to this need of exporters, the government of India has multiple schemes and programs in place. The most prominent of these are the market access initiative, the export promotion scheme, the export-import bank of India, and the Export Credit Guarantee Corporation.

The market access initiative provides exporters with resources for entering a new market. This includes providing financial assistance for trade shows, market research, and other market entry expenses. The export promotion scheme works to promote the exports of India as well as helps exporters to expand their business. It provides grants to exporters to help them explore new markets and develop export capability.

Export import bank of India provides exporters with access to long-term finance and export-oriented funding. It provides access to banking products such as foreign exchange, risk insurance, export credits, and export finance. The Export Credit Guarantee Corporation provides insurance to exporters against certain risks associated with export of goods and services. This helps exporters attain easy access to credit and reduces the cost of export for exporters.

In addition to these resources, the government of India also provides exporters with programs such as the Service Exports from India Scheme and the Barter System of International Trade. These programs provide exporters with various incentives to promote export operations.

The government of India provides numerous resources and support to exporters, ranging from financial assistance to risk insurance. These resources help exporters to explore new markets and achieve greater success. With increased access to resources and support, exporters in India have the growing potential to become global leaders in export operations.

CHAPTER TWENTY-THREE

GOVERNMENT SUPPORT AND RESOURCES FOR EXPORTERS

India is a rapidly growing economy, and the government has taken steps to ensure that exporters are able to take advantage of the opportunities available to them. The government provides a range of support and resources to exporters, including financial assistance, tax incentives, and access to export markets.

Financial assistance is available to exporters in the form of grants, loans, and other forms of credit. These funds can be used to cover the costs of production, marketing, and other expenses associated with exporting. Tax incentives are also available, such as reduced tariffs and duty-free imports. These incentives can help exporters to reduce their costs and increase their profits.

The government also provides access to export markets. This includes providing information on potential markets, helping exporters to find buyers, and providing assistance with the paperwork and regulations associated with exporting. The government also works to ensure that exporters are able to access the latest technology and resources to help them succeed in the global market.

In addition to the support and resources provided by the government, there are also a number of private organizations that provide assistance to exporters. These organizations can provide advice and guidance on the best practices for exporting, as well as access to networks of buyers and suppliers.

The government of India has taken steps to ensure that exporters are able to take advantage of the opportunities available to them. Through financial assistance, tax incentives, and access to export markets, the government has created an environment that is conducive to successful exporting. Private organizations also provide additional support and resources to exporters, helping them to succeed in the global market.

CHAPTER TWENTY-FOUR

CHALLENGES AND OPPORTUNITIES IN EXPORTING FROM INDIA

The concept of global trade has been gaining traction in recent years, especially in India. Not only does exporting bring immense economic benefits for Indian producers, but opportunities for growth and collaboration have also increased. This article will explore the various challenges and opportunities available to Indian exporters, in order to gain a better understanding of the sector.

One of the primary benefits of exporting from India is the immense market potential. With its rapidly rising population, low cost of labor, and abundance of natural resources and skilled workers, India is an ideal place to set up exporting businesses. Moreover, India has a large pool of qualified and experienced exporters which can easily supply products and services to other countries and take advantage of the world's global markets.

On the other hand, exporting from India is not without its risks. Firstly, Indian exporters must abide by the strict rules and regulations of the host countries they are exporting to. Additionally, if the products or services don't meet the standards of their target market, Indian exporters risk losing money and reputational damage. Furthermore, tariffs, customs, and currency fluctuations can lead to increased costs for Indian companies. Political instability and corruption in some countries can also put Indian exporters in a difficult situation.

There are many opportunities available to Indian exporters to capitalize on in order to offset these risks. Firstly, India has a strong position in the region, which gives it a competitive advantage compared to other countries. Additionally, many countries have preferential trade deals with India, allowing exporters to benefit from lower tariffs and other trade arrangements. Furthermore, a free-trade agreement between India and several countries in the region is set to come into effect in the near future, which will further reduce costs and facilitate trade. Finally, there are a number of initiatives and grants available to Indian exporters, which increase their access to global markets.

India offers tremendous potential for exporters, but also poses certain risks. Despite this, exporters can take advantage of the many opportunities available to them, such as preferential trade deals, free-trade agreements, and grants. By understanding the various challenges and opportunities faced by Indian exporters, businesses can navigate the market and realize their full exporting potential.

CHAPTER TWENTY-FIVE

CASE STUDIES AND SUCCESS STORIES

India is a country of immense potential, and its export sector is no exception. India has exported goods and services worth $314 billion in the financial year 2019-20, and further, export figures continue to rise. As such, the need to capitalize on the success stories that come out of the sector is important. Case studies and success stories of the export sector come in handy to allow budding entrepreneurs, investors and industry professionals to learn and take inspiration from, to strive towards more successes.

Case studies are an exemplary way of viewing success, where each of its aspects is broken down into smaller components and evaluated to draw conclusions. These serve as lessons, which can be adapted by entrepreneurs to suit their own business. Case studies help entrepreneurs uncover what works best for their sector of business, in terms of marketing, promotions or operations. Careful study of such cases and appending them to their own business plan can help them get success stories of their own.

For rookies, case studies and success stories serve as narrative guides, which provide the necessary facts and figures regarding the process, the decisions that were made, the success achieved, goals accomplished, and roadblocks faced. This helps one to make smarter decisions, especially when working in uncharted fields. Understanding the game-changers, process to becoming a market leader, and secrets to success enable individuals to make well-informed decisions while planning.

Analyze the strategies used by Indian exporters to achieve success in the global market.

Examine the challenges they faced and the solutions they implemented to overcome them.

Investigate the impact of these successes on the Indian economy and the potential for further growth.

Consider the lessons that can be learned from these case studies and success stories and how they can be applied to other export markets.

Finally, discuss the potential for India to become a major player in the global export market.

Case studies and success stories are essential in the international markets, especially in the context of export from India. For both rookies and industry experts, they serve not just as a means of inspiration but also guidelines to facilitate their success. They help individuals understand their industry better and identify the potential of their business. Thus, such case studies and success stories should be thoroughly analyzed and extracted to the maximum potential in order to use the wealth of knowledge to one's advantage.

Other Books Of The Author

1. The Moments When I Met God
2. Kashiyile Theertha Pathangal
3. GURU GYAN VANI
4. Abhiprerak Gita
5. ASSI SE JAIN GHAT TAK
6. Hopelessness of Arjuna
7. The Soul and It's True Nature
8. Sense of Action (Karma)
9. Action through Wisdom
10. Action through Wisdom
11. THEORY AND PRACTICAL OF EVERY ACTION
12. LOGICAL UNDERSTANDING OF THE SUPREME
13. THE IMPERISHABLE SUPREME
14. Yatra Nishadraj se Hanuman Ghat Tak
15. Yatra Karnatak Ghat se Raja Ghat Tak
16. Yatra Pandey Ghat se Prayagraj Ghat Tak
17. Yatra Ranjendra Prasad Ghat se Dattatreya Ghat Tak
18. YaatraSindhiya Ghat se Gwaliar Ghat Tak
19. Yatra Mangala Gauri Ghat se Hanuman Gadhi Ghat Tak
20. Yatra Gaay Ghat Se Nishad Ghat Tak
21. MAA GANGA, GHATEN EVM UTSAV
22. Ganga Arti Dev Deepavali evam Any Utsav
23. Potentials of Digitalized India
24. VEDIC CONSCIOUSNESS
25. A Brief Introduction to Vedic Science
26. Kashi ke Barah Jyotirling
27. IMPACT OF MOTIVATION
28. Let's have a Milky Way Journey
29. Color Therapy in a Nutshell

30. Rigveda in a Nutshell
31. Yajurveda in a Nutshell
32. Samveda in a Nutshell
33. Atharva Veda in a Nutshell
34. Ayushman Bhava - Ayurveda
35. Srimad Bhagavad Gita and Upanishad Connection
36. Srimad Bhagavad Gita - an attempt to summarize each chapter.
37. Facts and Impact of Nakshatra
38. Astro Gems - NAVARATNA
39. Ekadashi - A Concise Overview
40. A Concise View of Hanuman Chalisa
41. Inspirational Gita
42. Nakshatraranyam
43. Summary of 18 Mahapuranas
44. Synopsis of 18 Upa Puranas
45. Rigvediya Upanishads
46. Shukla Yajurvediya Upanishads
47. Krishna Yajurvediya Upanishads
48. Samavediya Upanishads
49. Atharvavediya Upanishads
50. The Seven Great Sages
51. From Rocket Scientist to President Dr. APJ Abdul Kalam
52. The Visionary's Voice - Quotes of Dr. APJ Abdul Kalam
53. The Wisdom of Swami Vivekananda: Insights and Inspiration from a Legendary Spiritual Teacher
54. Ayurvedic Remedies from the Garden
55. Sages and Seers
56. Rising Strong – Motivational Stories of Women
57. Beyond Flames -Mystery stories of Funeral Ghat Manikarnika
58. The Origins of Tulsi: A Look at the Mythological Roots of the Plant"

Contact

DR. JAGADEESH PILLAI

MBA & PhD in Vedic Science

Four Times Guinness World Record Holder

Winner of Mahatma Gandhi Vishwa Shanti Puraskar and
Global Peace Ambassador

Gemology, Astro & Vastu Consultant - Spiritual Counselor

Consultant for designing World Record Ideas

Efficient Tarot Card Reader

9839093003

myrichindia@gmail.com

drjagadeeshpillai@facebook

drjagadeeshpillai@instagram

jagadeeshpillai@youtube

www. JAGADEESHPILLAI.com

|| LOKAHA SAMASTHAHA SUKHINO BHAVANTU ||

www.ingramcontent.com/pod-product-compliance
Lightning Source LLC
Chambersburg PA
CBHW061702130726
47996CB00006B/2125